WIMBLEDON

VISIONS OF THE CHAMPIONSHIPS

WIMBLEDON

VISIONS OF THE CHAMPIONSHIPS

THE ALL ENGLAND LAWN TENNIS & CROQUET CLUB
EDITED BY IAN HEWITT AND BOB MARTIN

CONTENTS

Foreword by Tim Henman   6

Introduction by Philip Brook,
Chairman, The All England Lawn Tennis & Croquet Club   8

Acknowledgements   10

WIMBLEDON PREPARES   12

Courts of Champions   26

A CHAMPIONSHIPS DAY DAWNS   32

Serving The Championships   62

GATES OPEN, PLAY BEGINS   68

A Royal Visit   106

AFTERNOON PLAY   114

Rain and the Roof   180

EARLY EVENING TO DUSK   192

Finals Days   224

WIMBLEDON AT NIGHT   246

FOREWORD

I am delighted to support this book and I have much enjoyed viewing these wonderful images of Wimbledon.

I have very many great memories of my playing days at The Championships. It was always special to compete as a home player in what so many competitors consider to be the best and most prestigious tournament in the world.

I now enjoy new roles as a television commentator and as a member of the tournament's Committee of Management. Even more than before, I appreciate the unstinting efforts of so many people and different organisations who contribute to the success of The Championships. I have seen many changes, even during my time, as the All England Club continually strives to improve the facilities and experience for players, spectators and millions of viewers worldwide. Yet, in essence, nothing changes. Vitally, Wimbledon's atmosphere is unique and special every year.

The beautiful and striking photographs in this book instantly trigger memories of summer and the colour, excitement and variety of Wimbledon – the world's premier tennis event.

I hope you enjoy this book as much as I do.

Tim Henman OBE

(left) Tim Henman reaches wide during an exhibition match to celebrate the Centre Court's new retractable roof in May 2009, his last appearance on the Centre Court

INTRODUCTION

I am pleased, as Chairman of the All England Lawn Tennis & Croquet Club, to introduce this book which is published as we approach the 125th Championships.

Initiated by one of my colleagues on our Committee of Management, Ian Hewitt, it provides an excellent opportunity for us to showcase many fantastic images taken by the Club's photography team at The Championships, so ably led by Bob Martin. The photographs were all taken over the last two or three years and most during 2010's memorable tournament. They convey, vividly, the extraordinary range of people, happenings and activities that contribute to the overall 'Wimbledon experience' from dawn to dusk.

Last year, we were honoured that Her Majesty The Queen was able to attend and enjoy Wimbledon. The sun shone and the crowds were magnificent and joyful. It was a wonderful occasion. This year is also special as we celebrate the 125th Championships. This book, and its visions of The Championships, is part of that celebration – and a recognition of the efforts of so many organisations and individuals (a large number of whom are volunteers returning each year) who assist the Club and without whom The Championships would not be successful or, indeed, possible. We at the All England Club are grateful to them all.

I hope you enjoy the photographs in this book.

Philip Brook
Chairman, The All England
Lawn Tennis & Croquet Club

The All England Croquet Club was founded in 1868 and the first lawn tennis Championship meeting held in 1877. The Club's distinctive colours, dark green and purple, were introduced in 1909

ACKNOWLEDGEMENTS

I am struck every year by the range of 'experiences' enjoyed by spectators attending The Championships and by the many different groups of people who contribute to Wimbledon's unique atmosphere. I thought it would be a delight to celebrate The Championships by reflecting this diversity, from dawn to dusk, in an illustrated book.

I am grateful to the committee and many other colleagues at the All England Club for supporting this project. John Barrett has provided valuable guidance. Alan Little's 'Wimbledon Compendium' has, as ever, been the source of unrivalled information. My wife, Jenifer, has contributed many helpful ideas and contributions to the text. I also thank Vision Sports Publishing who, as publishers, have captured our vision with commitment and imagination.

The principal contributors to the book's content have, of course, been the Club's outstanding team of photographers at The Championships, led by Bob Martin. They have produced a glorious array of images reflecting the magic of Wimbledon. This is their work.

Ian Hewitt

I have for many years enjoyed leading a team of photographers at The Championships on behalf of the All England Club. Every year, we aim to produce the best images of the action to meet the Club's requirements.

Last year, we were delighted to have the opportunity of taking even more varied photographs with a view to conveying Wimbledon's special atmosphere for this book. We needed little encouragement. These are images we love taking. All in a year when the Queen also visited The Championships!

The photographs in this book are the work of this team. I have been pleased to participate but my particular thanks go to my colleagues: Tom Lovelock, Matthias Hangst, Chris Raphael and Neil Tingle together with Professional Sport's Tommy Hindley, John Buckle and Steve Wake. They are a terrific group of professionals. I am grateful to the All England Club for the pleasure of working with this team and on this project. I hope you enjoy the images.

Bob Martin

WIMBLEDON
PREPARES

The Week Before The Championships

The grounds of Wimbledon are bustling with activity in the days leading up to The Championships. Carefully orchestrated by the team at the All England Club, pieces fall into place with well-established custom and precision. Yet, tradition at Wimbledon is accompanied by innovation and each year there will invariably be something new; perhaps a new court, facility or supporting technology.

For the players: match courts are finely prepared, ball boys and girls go through their final training routines, electronic scoreboards are tested, practice courts are full, accommodation and transport are arranged, the draw is made and early press interviews are held. For the spectators: final touches of painting are completed around the grounds, hanging baskets and hydrangeas appear, catering areas are cleaned and prepared, staff are trained, stewards are instructed, shops are stocked and chairs and benches are put into position. For the viewers: broadcasting cables and connections are installed, television camera positions are checked and equipment assembled, broadcasters, press and photographers arrive for accreditation. And much, much more...

Planning for The Championships is a year-round activity. It is, though, in the days and weeks approaching the tournament that the physical pieces come together like a giant jigsaw. Teamwork is key. The theatre for one of the world's great sporting events is being prepared for action.

(previous page) The finishing touches are applied to Centre Court

(right) Annual weeding of the water garden is no light task. The view is from the northern end of Aorangi Terrace, popularly known as Henman Hill, with St Mary's Church in the distance. The grounds for The Championships, including the Club's car parks, total around 42 acres

A last touch of paint is applied
around the grounds, including
(above) the barriers in front of
the entrance to the Clubhouse
where, on finals days,
spectators will gather to greet
the newly-crowned champions

Sweeping and cleaning with a difference, including **(top right)** beneath the 75 Lloyd Loom wicker chairs of the Royal Box in Centre Court

(above and right) 450 players or more, of approximately 70 different nationalities, compete in the five main draw events at The Championships. There are 128 players in the draw for the men's and ladies' singles and 64 pairs in the men's and ladies' doubles, with 48 pairs for the mixed doubles. This keeps staff busy, before and during the tournament, preparing the results boards around the grounds

(above) Approximately 1,500 flowering hydrangea plants, specially grown in the UK, are a familiar feature

Training is hard but pride is considerable for Wimbledon's 250 ball boys and girls. They are selected, amid considerable competition, from local schools and participants in the All England Club's junior tennis programme. The successful applicants receive intensive training from February onwards. They are a distinctive and well-loved sight on the courts at Wimbledon

The Championships

Practice Clothing on Championships Courts

Players are reminded that the rule:

"ALMOST ENTIRELY WHITE"
and
"ACCEPTABLE TENNIS ATTIRE"

applies to:
ANY PERSON PLAYING AT ALL TIMES

PLEASE NOTE:
Players not conforming to this rule will be asked to leave the court.

Referee's Office

There are 22 practice courts in Aorangi Park to the north-east of the grounds. They are regularly in use in the period up to and during The Championships. Daily practice, under the watchful eye of coaches and trainers, is an important routine even for great players. Roger Federer **(top right)** is keen not to miss his allotted time. Andy Murray **(left)** enjoys a lighter moment. White clothing, at least during the tournament, is a firm Wimbledon tradition

COURTS OF CHAMPIONS

Wimbledon has no more distinctive feature than its grass courts. The Championships are unique – alone of the four Grand Slams, they are played on grass.

No other tennis tournament has a longer or prouder tradition. Initiated in 1877, The Championships have been held on the same grounds since 1922. These are courts on which, since then, all the great champions of the game have played – from Bill Tilden and Suzanne Lenglen to Rafael Nadal and Serena Williams.

Each year the highest quality playing surface must be produced for the world's best players to display their full range of shots. With 19 tournament courts and 22 practice courts,

care and maintenance is a full-time task. The Head Groundsman leads a team of 18 permanent ground staff increasing with temporary staff to around 30 for the period of The Championships. Sown with perennial rye grass, the courts are cut to a height of 8mm for tournament play. All courts are mown, rolled and re-lined daily during The Championships.

No grass courts are better known. No lawns in the country receive more careful or caring attention.

The quality of the courts is vital. Surface hardness of all courts is measured daily (above), and (right) all courts are mown every morning during The Championships with loving care to their tournament height of 8mm

All courts are rolled and re-lined daily during
The Championships – that is nearly two miles
of lines to be marked on the tournament courts
alone! A white compound containing china
clay is used. Baselines are marked to a width
of 100mm, other lines to a width of 50mm, all
with precision

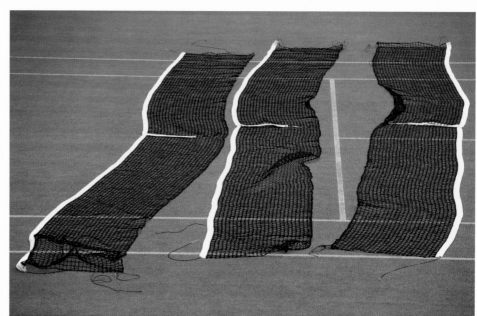

Nets are unrolled, checked and fitted, perfectly. Centre Court and Court 1 are set up for singles play with side-posts repositioned, and wider nets used, for any doubles events

A CHAMPIONSHIPS
DAY DAWNS

6 am - 10.30 am

It is around 6am. Overnight queuers in Wimbledon Park are awoken by the stewards and by morning's sunrise. Tents are packed away. The Chief Steward arrives on his bicycle to supervise the day ahead. Many of his team have worked through the night and are ready for a well-deserved breakfast. The Queue grows in its thousands. The mood is lively and full of anticipation. As early light dawns, the Wimbledon day is well underway.

Fresh food stocks have been arriving, including the strawberries from Kent. The caterers prepare for a busy day. Security staff undertake a diligent search of the grounds; sniffer dogs are hard at work. Rufus the hawk shows his fearsome skills, warning the local pigeons not to enter the Centre Court.

The Head Groundsman checks the weather forecast. Instructions are given to deflate and remove the court covers. The grass is mown, the hardness of the soil checked and the lines rewhitened. Umpires and officials report for duty. Ball boys and girls arrive for their day's work. The Referee and his team check the playing schedules.

While thousands of ticket-holders make their way to London SW19 and before a single ball is struck, much is happening at the All England Club.

(previous page) The weather vane positioned above Café Pergola near Church Road searches for the day's wind conditions. It was presented to the Club by a former Club Chairman, Sir Brian Burnett

(right) Early morning sun catches the entrance gates in Church Road. The Championships, as from the beginning in 1877, are staged under the auspices of the All England Lawn Tennis & Croquet Club

(right) An early security check is made along the main pathway, known as St Mary's Walk. The view here is from the north with St Mary's Church prominent in the distance

(far right) Catering areas are cleaned and prepared for another busy day. Wimbledon is the largest single annual sporting catering operation carried out in Europe. Around 1,800 catering staff are employed

Rufus, a Harris hawk, discourages local pigeons from entering Centre Court by his presence **(right)** on the fixed roof of Centre Court and **(far right)** inside the retractable roof. He flies, under the supervision of Avian Control, for one hour every morning during The Championships before the gates open

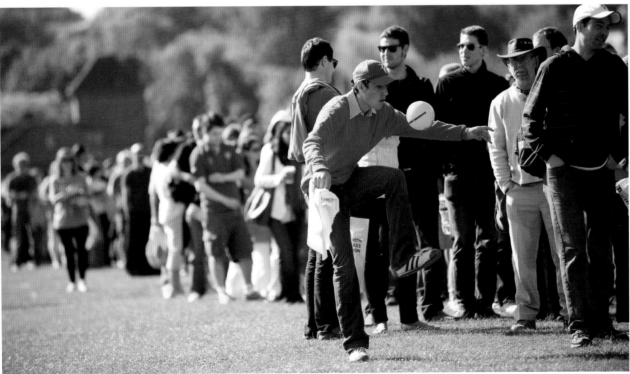

People queuing in Wimbledon Park, many camping overnight, wait patiently for the gates to open. Although demand for tickets invariably exceeds supply, in a unique policy among the Grand Slams, approximately 6,000 ground tickets are reserved for sale to the public on the day (along with around 1,500 show court tickets during each of the first nine days)

Police sniffer dogs enjoy their early morning task. The Metropolitan Police and the Club work in close co-operation before and during the tournament

Over 28,000 kilos of strawberries, mostly from Kent, are consumed during The Championships. With fresh deliveries arriving every morning, 'hulling' and preparation is an early daily task

(overleaf) Court coverers unveil Wimbledon's grass courts for the day's action. Around 160 are engaged during The Championships

Jelena JANKOVIC
Regina KULIKOVA
Ajla TOMLJANOVIC
Karolina SPREM
Evgeniya RODINA
Vera ZVONAREVA
Venus WILLIAMS

Simon ASPELIN / Paul HANLEY
Julien BENNETEAU / Michael LLODRA
Mahesh BHUPATHI / Max MIRNYI
Frantisek CERMAK / Michal MERTINAK
Lukas DLOUHY / Leander PAES
Chris EATON / Dominic INGLOT
Mardy FISH / Mark KNOWLES
Marcel GRANOLLERS / Tommy ROBREDO
Jan HAJEK / Rainer SCHUETTLER
John ISNER / Sam QUERREY
Akgul AMANMURADOVA / Kristina BARROIS
Timea BACSINSZKY / Tathiana GARBIN
Jill CRAYBAS / Marina ERAKOVIC
Eleni DANIILIDOU / Jasmin WOEHR
Sara ERRANI / Roberta VINCI
Sophie FERGUSON / Maria IRIGOYEN
Andrea HLAVACKOVA / Lucie HRADECKA
Jelena JANKOVIC / Chanelle SCHEEPERS
Anne KEOTHAVONG / Melanie SOUTH
Vesna MANASIEVA

Julian KNOWLE / Andy RAM
Jesse LEVINE / Ryan Sweeting
Wesley MOODIE / Dick NORMAN
Marcelo MELO / Bruno SOARES
Daniel NESTOR / Nenad ZIMONJIC
Michal PRZYSIEZNY / Dudi SELA
Stephane ROBERT / Rogier WASSEN
Rik DE VOEST / Mischa ZVEREV
Nina BRATCHIKOVA / Vitalia DIATCHENKO
Monica NICULESCU / Shahar PEER
Lilia OSTERLOH / Anna TATISHVILI
Sally PEERS / Laura ROBSON
Jocelyn RAE / Heather WATSON
Lucie SAFAROVA / Vera ZVONAREVA
Elena VESNINA / Aleksandra WOZNIAK
Edina GALLOVITS / Klaudia JANS

More than 650 matches are played in all events during The Championships – and that means work not only for the players and court officials but also many behind the scenes preparing for the day's matches

Courts are mown and re-lined daily, while court coverers – after completing their early morning tasks – take an impromptu rest. The ivy-clad frontage of Centre Court **(far left)** provides a splendid backdrop to the work

Teams of racket stringers are constantly at work, with each player's rackets having precise specifications, including **(right)** those of Rafael Nadal. Wooden rackets have not been used by players at Wimbledon since 1987

Towels are unpacked and prepared for the matches, with different designs for ladies and men. Towels continue to be one of the best-selling items of Wimbledon merchandise and more than 32,000 were sold to the public in 2010 through the Club's retail and online shops

Preparation is constant. Programmes are on sale each day, updated with the previous day's results. Broadcasting cables and microphones are checked. Ice is packed ready for each court. Members of the police (far right) also take a close interest in the day's programme

Wimbledon Tennis
THE CHAMPIONSHIPS
WIMBLEDON
sportsworld.co.uk
SPORTSWORLD
making great events better
01235 555844

The Queue has become a Wimbledon institution. When the ground capacity (38,500 in 2011) is reached, ground entry is on the basis of 'one out, one in'. The Queue is supervised, efficiently but gently, by the Honorary Stewards

The Queue stretches through Wimbledon Park, passes through security checks on the grounds of Wimbledon Park Golf Club and comes across the temporary bridge over Church Road to arrive at the entry turnstiles. Total attendances during The Championships in recent years have been around 500,000 with daily attendances in the first week frequently reaching 40,000 and more

SERVING THE CHAMPIONSHIPS

The staging of The Championships depends on a large network of officials and staff, approaching 5,000 in number, engaged for the duration of the tournament – from stewards to ball boys and girls, ground staff to court officials and attendants, security guards to house-keeping staff, transport service drivers to dressing room attendants, buildings personnel to catering staff, lift operators to left-luggage attendants, press staff to physiotherapists, and many more. All play an important role.

The Honorary and Service Stewards, in particular, are one of Wimbledon's most distinctive and welcome sights. The Honorary Stewards (around 190 volunteers recruited from the ordinary public) marshal the queues inside and outside the ground, including the overnight Queue, and act as 'hosts' to the arriving public. They are assisted by more than 300 servicemen and women, again all volunteers, on leave from the Armed Forces (many having served on recent active duty abroad) together with a contingent of around 200 volunteers from the London Fire Brigade.

The uniforms, efficiency and gentle authority of these Honorary and Service Stewards provide a unique and much-loved feature of Wimbledon.

Hats and uniforms of the Service Stewards provide a colourful and reassuring sight around Wimbledon. Proud to serve their country, they are all volunteers at The Championships. A large majority keenly return each year

About 190 volunteer stewards, members of the Association of Wimbledon Honorary Stewards, have a distinctive and vital presence at The Championships. A large majority of Honorary Stewards return each year for this important role. Here, several enjoy the morning sun as they listen to instructions for the day

More than 5,000 staff are engaged during the fortnight to support the staging of The Championships, including approximately 1,800 catering staff, nearly 200 ground staff and court attendants, more than 200 house-keeping staff and around 75 night cleaners. For many students, it is a welcome but demanding two weeks with a difference. (far left) Catering staff enjoy a moment's relaxation, and (above) 15,000 seats on Centre Court are prepared for the day

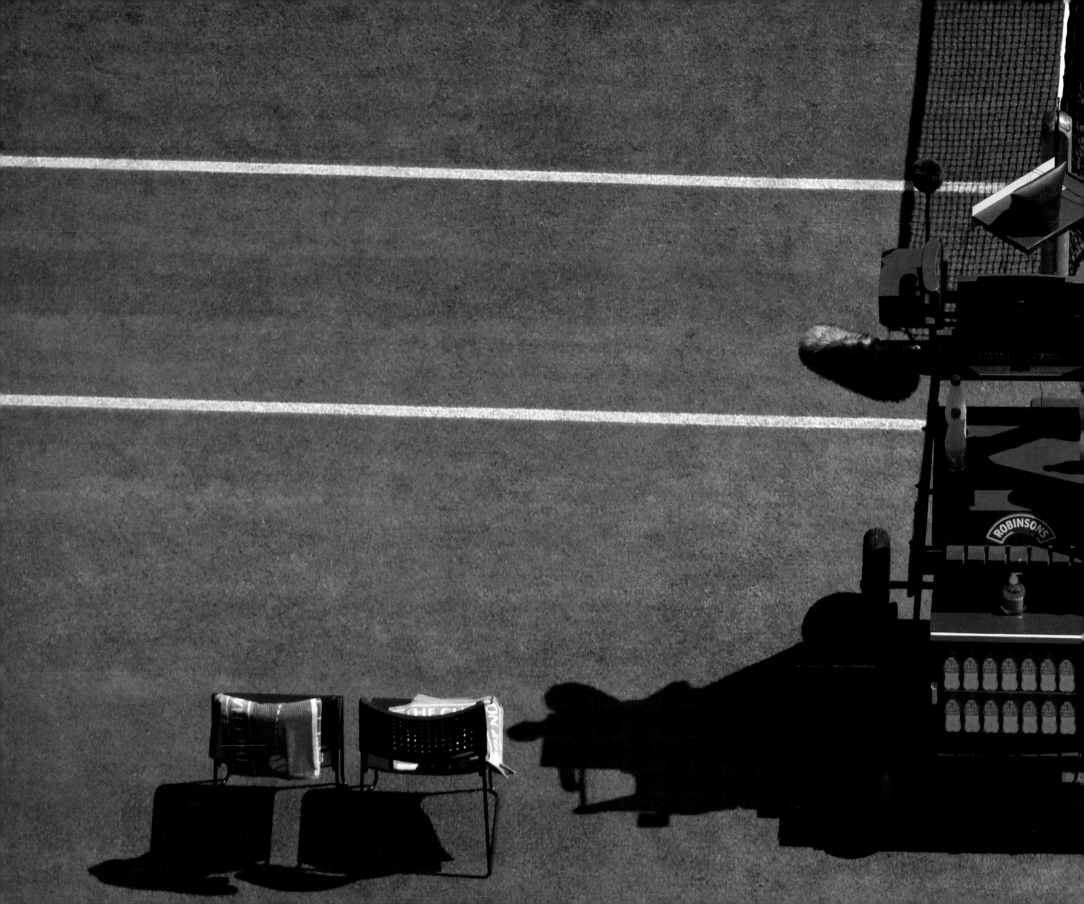

GATES OPEN,
PLAY BEGINS

10.30am-1pm

It is 10.30am. "Would the stewards please open the gates now. Thank you." Security staff lead the initial ranks of enthusiastic spectators into the main concourse. Those first in the Queue gain their reward – newly-purchased show court tickets – and others purposefully head to their favourite viewing positions. At few major sporting events around the world can fans be so close to the scene of play as at Wimbledon.

By the courts, the smell of freshly-mown grass is in the air. Lines are still being marked and nets are being raised. Players are arriving, many in the courtesy cars provided, others walking from houses nearby. The Aorangi practice courts are busy with players (and their coaches) going through final drills.

The day's play has been planned – but which matches will be short, which will be long? Will there be another marathon? Stewards are in position around the courts. At midday, all courts (except Centre Court and Court 1) are occupied by players and officials. Wimbledon is ready for play.

Outside, the Queue still stretches out. The last few of the initial thousands gain entry before the grounds reach capacity and the turnstiles close. Others wait, patiently and optimistically, to gain entry later in the day. Around the grounds at the All England Club, all is vibrant.

(previous page) The courts have been 'dressed'. Lines, seats, towels and umpire's chair have all been prepared and are ready for the day's opening matches

WELCOME TO THE
CHAMPIONSHIPS 2010

THE CHAMPIONSHIPS
WIMBLEDON

At 10.30am the gates open
to the waiting thousands
outside, although several
hundred on-day buyers of
tickets from the Queue are
allowed to enter, at around
9.30am, to form an initial
'corral' inside the grounds

(right) Security staff wait for the 10.30am instruction to proceed, just in time for strawberries to be delivered to the food outlets

(far right) Hundreds of fans in the early 'corral' are led through the main concourse before being 'released' to find their favourite positions. Around 700 security guards are engaged on all duties for The Championships

(left) Spectators flock along
the main concourse while
members look on from
Centre Court's balconies

(above left) Programme sellers
are busy, and (above right)
one spectator shows personal
support for her favourite player
from Switzerland

The grounds at Wimbledon cover, in total, more than 40 acres. Signage helps direct spectators to facilities which include numerous catering outlets, a pharmacy, retail shops, information kiosks, a bank, a museum and, most importantly, 19 tournament courts

(right) Umpires and court officials prepare for the day. There are around 330 in total, approximately 260 of whom are members of the Association of British Tennis Officials (ABTO), with the remaining officials coming from all over the world. These include a team of six ITF/Grand Slam chair umpires who officiate at all the Grand Slams

(far right) Ball boys and girls are ready for action. The ratio of boys to girls is approximately 50:50

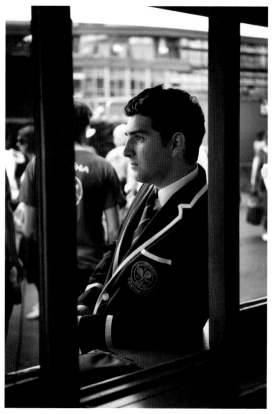

Players are on court at 12 noon on the outside
courts (unless previous bad weather has required
an earlier start to catch up on any backlog of
matches). The chair umpire spins the coin to
decide who serves first. Play begins

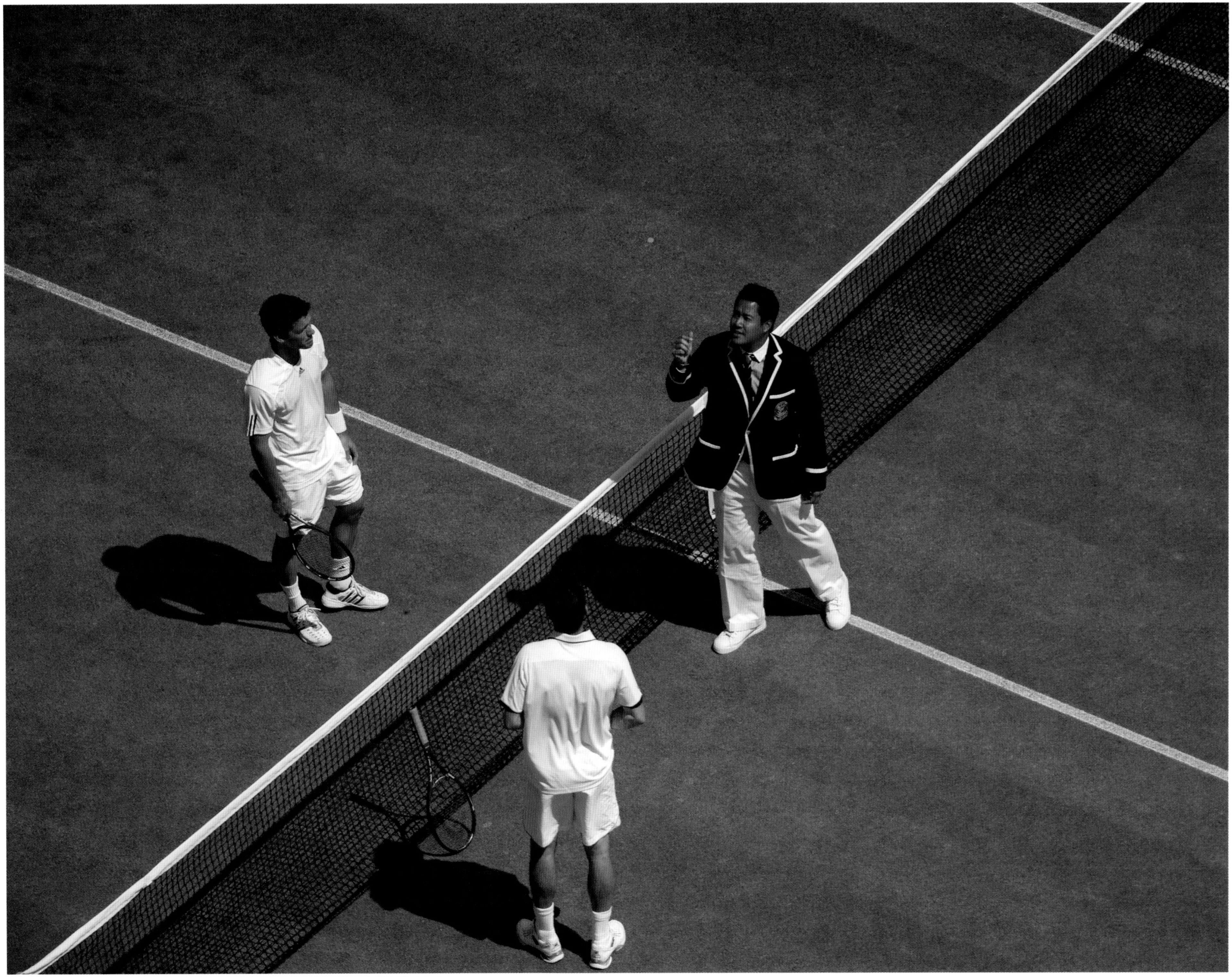

Balls are stored in a courtside refrigerator at 68°F and opened before play and at each scheduled change (after the first seven games and then every nine games). Approximately 54,250 balls are used during The Championships. Yellow balls have been used since 1986

(right) The umpire rules from on high

(far right) The outside courts are active with matches in all events as the fortnight progresses. More than 170 matches are played in the three main doubles events alone during The Championships. To the left, preparatory work can be seen on Court 4 which will be in play in 2011, alongside a new Court 3 which will seat 2,000 spectators

(right) Britain's Laura
Robson hits hard, and
(far right) a lineswoman
signals that a shot is in

Spectators enjoy the morning sunshine and plan their next moves. There are approximately 650 hanging baskets around the grounds at Wimbledon

(overleaf left) A packed crowd, taking advantage of all viewing positions, watches an extraordinary marathon on Court 18 in 2010 between John Isner and Nicolas Mahut, won eventually by Isner 70-68 in the fifth set. It is the longest match ever played in a leading tennis tournament

(overleaf right) There are few major sporting events where spectators get as close to the action as at Wimbledon. Here matches are in play at the southern end of the grounds

(right) The Referee, Andrew Jarrett, calmly and thoughtfully reviews progress of the day's proceedings. Approximately 650 matches are played throughout the fortnight (with around 365 in the first week). It is the Referee's task to schedule them and ensure, as far as is possible, that The Championships are completed on time

(far right) A police sniffer dog, his tasks complete, enjoys a fine view of the action on Court 18

Every vantage point is
secured to get a peek of
a popular match

(far left) On the two finals days, a band entertains spectators on Aorangi Terrace for an hour before moving across to Centre Court. Here, it is the Central Band of the Royal British Legion

(left) In recent years on the first Saturday and final Sunday, a one-hour demonstration has been given on Court 14 before play by a number of children in the Wimbledon Junior Tennis Initiative programme with participants from many local schools. The All England Club's coach, Dan Bloxham, takes them through their paces and Tim Henman gives encouragement and advice

Centre Court - South West Hall

Lunchtime offers many different experiences around the grounds. **(top)** Club members take in the splendid view from one of the Clubhouse balconies. **(above)** Guests in hospitality marquees, some very well-known, enjoy pre-afternoon refreshment. **(above right)** A number of spectators find a welcoming bench for rest and nourishment

(right) Aorangi Terrace is a popular spot for many to enjoy a summer's day

(left) Spectators watch the action on Court 19, at the northern end of the grounds, as Regina Kulikova serves in the midday sunshine

(far left) Matches are in play across the courts at the southern end of the grounds

Security staff escort players to and from their matches. **(right)** Russia's Anna Kournikova (playing in the ladies' invitation doubles) is still popular and **(far right)** France's men's-seeded player Gael Monfils has many admirers

A ROYAL VISIT

The Royal Box has been a focus of attention ever since the days when King George V and Queen Mary were avid spectators. The Duke of Kent, as President of the All England Club and The Championships, attends regularly – and is frequently joined by other members of the Royal Family.

Wimbledon was honoured in 2010 by a visit from Her Majesty The Queen. Passing through the happy crowds, she met representatives of many different groups who contribute to The Championships: from spectators to stewards; from ball boys and girls to umpires; from youngsters in the Club's junior tennis programme to champions of the game. Roger Federer was immaculate in white shirt, suit and

All England Club tie.

The Queen took her rightful place in the Royal Box to the welcome of the Centre Court crowd. Britain's leading player, Andy Murray, performed with distinction. It was a special occasion and one that we can recall through images of that magical day.

The sun shone and Wimbledon presented itself in a manner fit for a Queen.

(left) The Queen passes through the crowds along St Mary's Walk in 2010 before entering the Members Enclosure where (above and right), watched by players, members and the public, she is introduced to many leading players including the previous year's champions, Serena Williams and Roger Federer. This was the Queen's third visit to Wimbledon, and her first since 1977

COURT 5

| Gentlemen's Singles 2nd Rd |
| Martin FISCHER |
| Thomaz BELLUCCI |
| Ladies' Singles 2nd Rd |
| Daniela HANTUCHOVA |
| Barbora ZAHLAVOV |
| Gentlemen's Singles 2nd Rd |
| Philipp PETZSCHNER |
| Lukasz KUBOT |
| Ladies' Doubles 1st Rd |
| M. KONDRA/V. UHLIRO |
| C. BLACK/D. HANTUCHOVA |

COURT 6

| Gentlemen's Doubles 1st Rd |
| R. HUTCHINS/J. KERR |
| A. BOGDAN/A. SLABIN |
| Gentlemen's Doubles 1st Rd |
| D. NESTOR/N. ZIMONJIC |
| J. MARRAY/J. MURRAY |
| Ladies' Doubles 1st Rd |
| A. MEDINA/I. SENOGL |
| J. JANKOV/C. SCHEEP |
| Mixed Doubles 1st Rd |
| D. NORMAN/Y. WICKMAYER |
| J. MARRAY/A. SMITH |

COURT 7

| Gentlemen's Doubles 1st Rd |
| M. BHUPATHI/M. MIRNYI |
| M. GONZALEZ/S. PRIETO |
| Ladies' Doubles 1st Rd |
| E. VESNINA/V. ZVONAREVA |
| M. KORYTT/D. KUSTOV |
| Gentlemen's Doubles 1st Rd |
| G. GARCIA/A. MONTAN |
| S. ASPELIN/P. HANLEY |
| Ladies' Doubles 1st Rd |
| M. NICULESCU/S. PEER |
| A. BONDAR/K. BONDAR |

The Queen, accompanied by the Club Chairman, Tim Phillips, passes over the bridge from the Members Enclosure to Centre Court as joyful crowds of amateur photographers record the special moment

(overleaf) The Queen takes her place on Centre Court before enjoying a second-round match between Britain's Andy Murray and Finland's Jarkko Nieminen

After the match, the Queen views the southern end of the grounds from the Clubhouse balcony with the Club Chairman, Tim Phillips, before (right) meeting Andy Murray and Jarkko Nieminen

(far right) Before leaving, the Queen is presented in the entrance hall with replicas of the two singles trophies as a gift from the Club. The Duke of Kent, who is the Club's President and the Queen's cousin, is in attendance along with the Club Chairman, Tim Phillips. The men's singles trophy glistens in the nearby cabinet

1pm-6pm

At 1pm, with clockwork precision, the players walk out on to the perfect green lawns of the Centre Court and Court 1. Applause rings out for the white-clothed contestants. The spectators, eager and expectant, are ready.

The umpires are in position. Ball boys and girls, well-trained and regimental, wear their distinctive uniforms. The photographers are in their pits. Television cameras and commentators commence the day's coverage. Hawk-Eye awaits its first call to action. Up on Aorangi Terrace, on-day buyers of ground tickets are already watching 'the big screen' and enjoying the day. Now, the main spectacle of play on the two principal show courts begins.

On the outside courts, early matches are already being completed. For some players, the tournament has ended; for others, planning starts for the next round. As the fortnight progresses, different events and new players appear alongside main-draw singles still to be contested. Many doubles matches, fast and furious, take place and then it is time for the juniors (a number of whom will become famous in years to come) as well as the invited seniors (many famous names of the past, still skilful and sharp if not quite so athletic).

It is a glorious summer's afternoon at Wimbledon.

(previous page) A wide-angled lens captures an afternoon contest between Jan Hajek and Andy Murray before a capacity crowd of nearly 11,400 on Court 1 under a clear blue sky

(right) Roger Federer, as the previous year's singles champion, greets the crowd on the first day of The Championships in 2010

Roger Federer is at full stretch
during the opening match on
Centre Court in 2010. Just
visible are initial footmarks
of the players on the pristine
court. A friendly ladies'
doubles, among members of
the Club, 'plays in' the court
on the Saturday before
The Championships but,
otherwise, no play takes
place on Centre Court before
the tournament

(left) Roger Federer is
framed in the afternoon
sunshine

(above left) Hats are given
to fortunate guests in
the Royal Box and (above
right) the shade of an
umbrella is provided for the
players at change of ends

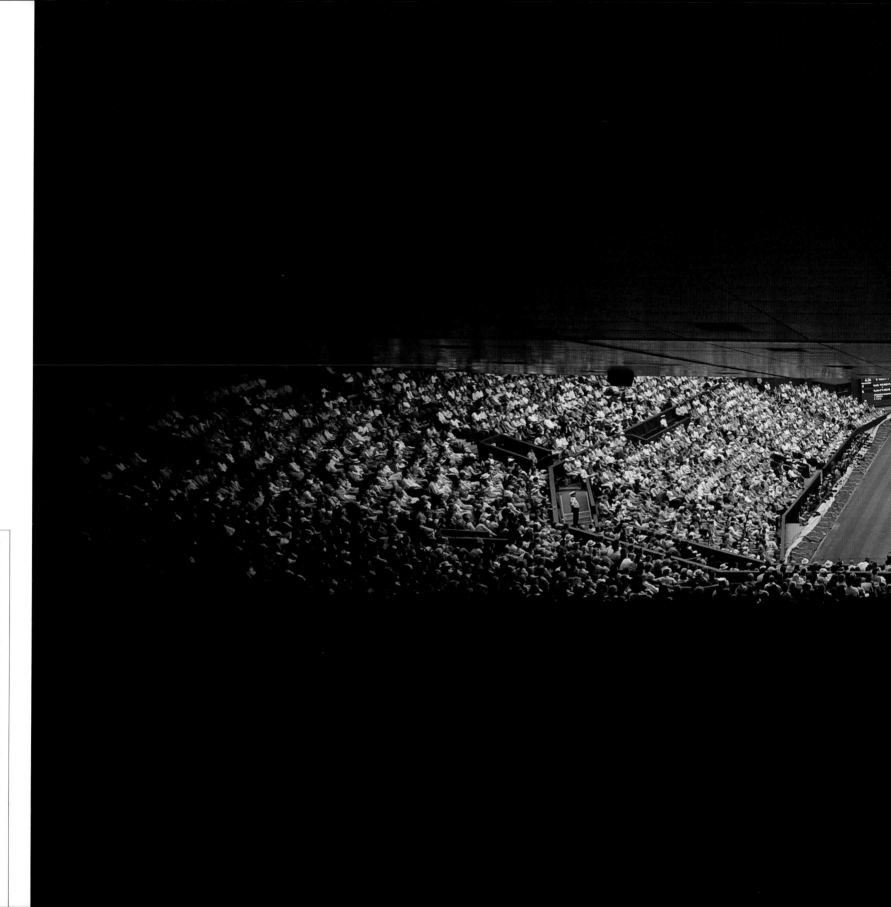

Spectators at the back of Centre Court focus on the drama below as Rafael Nadal serves before a capacity crowd of 15,000 in the sport's most famous arena. The construction of the retractable roof for 2009 involved the replacement of the fixed perimeter roof. The 12-sided shape of this roof, and its inward slope, reinstated the original design of Stanley Peach, the architect of Centre Court on the Club's move to Church Road in 1922

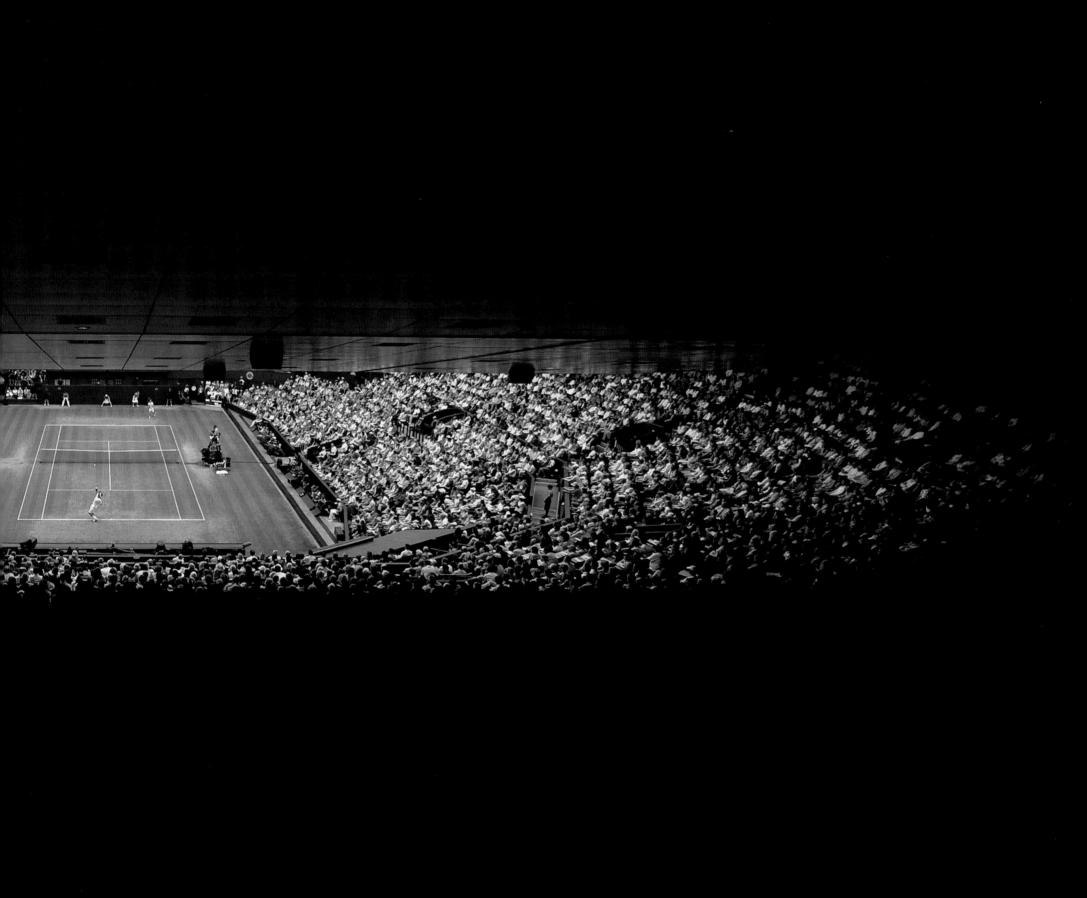

Three leading men at
full stretch: **(far left)**
Novak Djokovic, **(above)**
Andy Roddick and **(left)**
Jo-Wilfried Tsonga

The Royal Box is always a special place. **(top left)** Film stars Ben Stiller and Michael Caine are among the guests enjoying the occasion. A number of sporting stars are introduced to the crowd on the first Saturday including, in 2010, **(far left)** former tennis favourites Jan Kodes, Ilie Nastase and Martina Navratilova and **(left)** Evonne Goolagong-Cawley

(above) No warmer applause rang around the Centre Court in 2010 than, on Armed Forces Day, for representatives of the Armed Forces. Here, leading representatives responsible for the Service Stewards receive heartfelt applause on behalf of their colleagues

Three leading ladies in determined mood: **(left)** Vera Zvonareva, **(centre)** Kim Clijsters and **(right)** Caroline Wozniacki

(overleaf) The camera captures a framed, panoramic view of play on Court 1 with the linesmen and a capacity crowd of nearly 11,400 showing full concentration. Robert Kendrick is playing Jo-Wilfried Tsonga

The chair umpire rules. There are around 330 court officials at The Championships. Chair umpires normally take charge of two matches a day. Linesmen and women work in teams, two teams being assigned to each court. The teams work on a timed rotation, 75 minutes on and 75 minutes off

Improvement to the grounds and facilities are constant. **(above)** A new Court 2, seating approximately 4,000 spectators, was opened for play in 2009. It has its own intimate atmosphere with fans **(far right)** enjoying the afternoon sun

(overleaf) Belgium's Xavier Malisse watches the moving crowd as a Mexican wave takes place during a break in play on Court 1

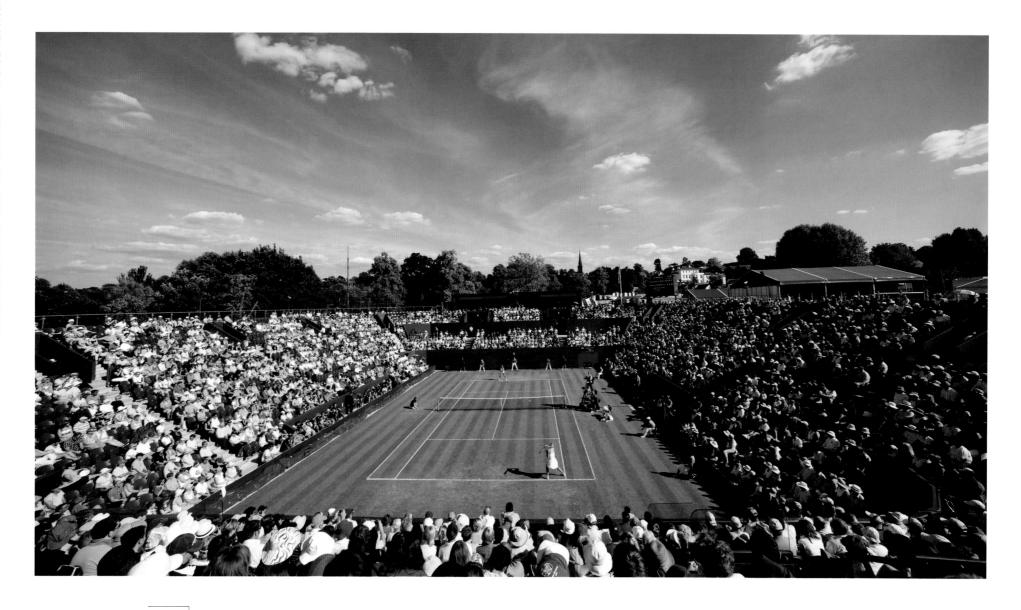

The outside courts are full of action. **(above)** Another view of Court 2. **(right)** A scene of the southern end of the grounds with spectators able to enjoy a close-up view of the action

(overleaf left) Court 18 is packed with spectators. **(overleaf right)** Others keep a watchful, if unconventional, view

(right and below) Cameras catch other celebrities enjoying the day. Film stars Colin Firth and Kim Cattrall are spotted

(far right) The Championships are the world's most widely seen tennis tournament, broadcast to more than 175 countries. Approximately 2,000 accreditations are processed each year for television and radio personnel. Sue Barker, Tim Henman and John McEnroe, now well-known television personalities, take a close-up view of scenes of former glory

(above left and right)
Former champions
Jimmy Connors and
Martina Navratilova
have television duties

(right) Andy Roddick
gives an early interview

(far right) A cockpit of television monitors in the Broadcast Centre displays action from around the grounds. Vision and audio signals are received from nine show courts, together with many other camera feeds, and distributed to all broadcasters. Television coverage was available in 2010 to more than three-quarters of a billion homes worldwide

(overleaf left) The graceful Maria Sharapova on Centre Court

(overleaf right) Ground staff keep a watchful eye on proceedings. If called into action in the event of rain, they take around 28 seconds to cover Centre Court. A court cover is still used, in the event of rain, while the retractable roof is being closed

14:39:16

FIBRE 1   FIBRE 2

CRT 1 BTY

CRT 16

CRT 17

CRT 18

Wimbledon
THE CHAMPIONSHIPS WIMBLEDON 1

PRESS 1   PRESS 2

CRT 2

CRT 5

CRT 12

CRT 14

PLAYERS

PGM AUX

PROGRAM

PREVIEW

ME 1

ME 2

ME 3

TURBO

CAM 3

Serena Williams (left) and
Anna Kournikova (above)
have distinctive features
which are readily recognisable

Umbrellas and parasols provide welcome shade for spectators and players alike on a hot, sunny afternoon

(overleaf left) A match ends on Court 1 with a player customarily throwing a gift to the crowd – but not usually his shoe. The player is Robert Kendrick after his match with Jo-Wilfried Tsonga

As the fortnight progresses, the doubles events provide considerable afternoon interest on the outside courts. **(left)** American twins Bob and Mike Bryan celebrate in their unique style. Behind them, with a perfect view, Royal Box guests for the day commence tea on the central Clubhouse balcony. **(above)** Venus and Serena Williams show sisterly determination and teamwork

In the second week, 'senior' stars of the game can be seen in the various invitational doubles events. **(left)** Former champion Goran Ivanisevic entertains the crowd in a lighter moment

(above) Jana Novotna and nine-time singles champion Martina Navratilova are still fiercely competitive

(overleaf) American Sam Querrey leaves sun for shade at the back of Centre Court as he reaches for a wide forehand in a late afternoon match

Hawk-Eye line technology has been used on the principal show courts since 2007, providing clarity and entertainment. High cameras around the court, carefully calibrated, relay the flight of the ball to a computer which reconstructs its trajectory. A control room **(right)** checks the shot and the result. **(far right)** Roger Federer awaits the verdict

(overleaf) Late afternoon is, for many, a time for refreshment. Members of the public fill the Pimm's and Champagne Bar. Over 200,000 glasses of Pimm's and 20,000 bottles of champagne are served throughout the grounds during the fortnight

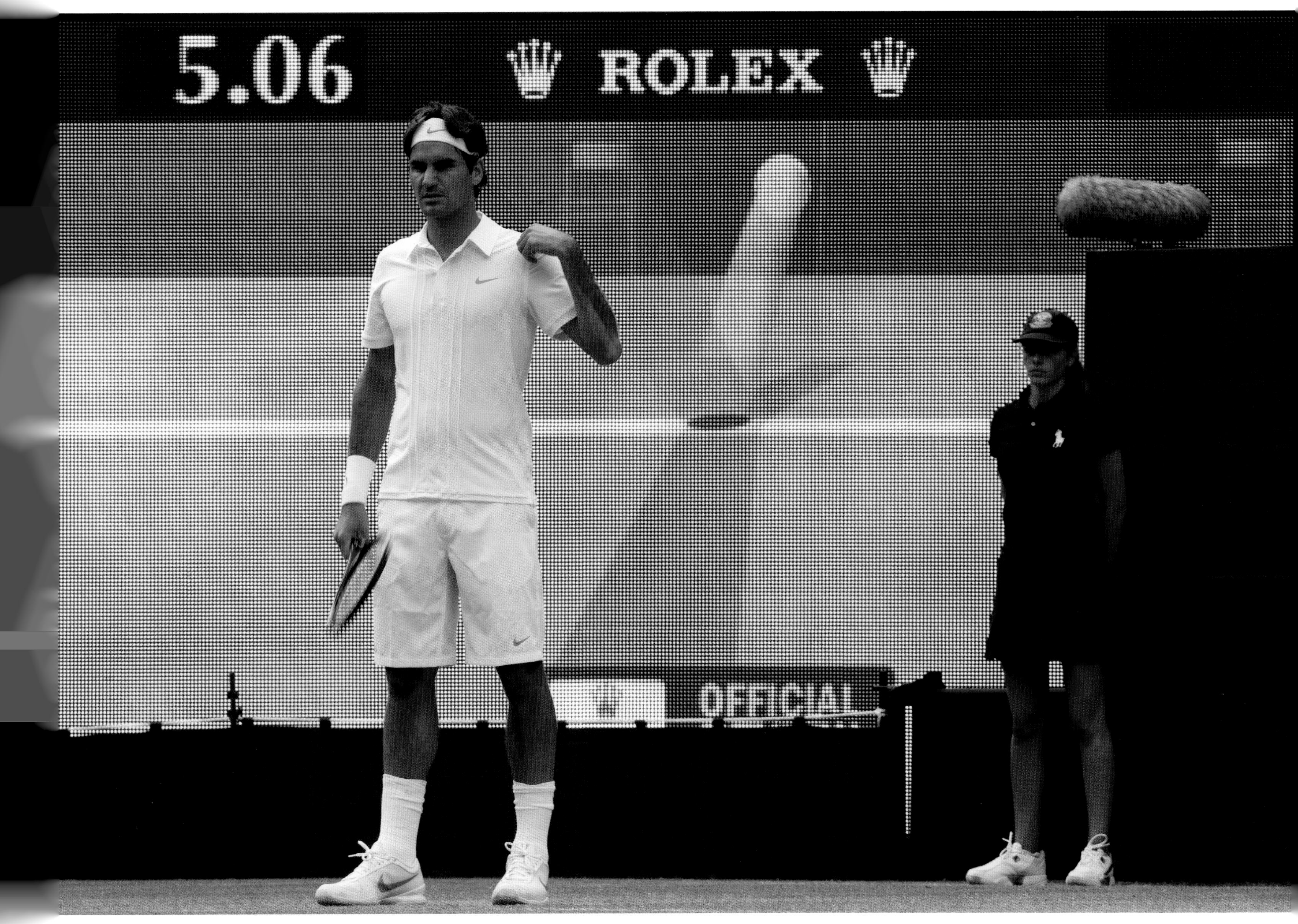
5.06
ROLEX
OFFICIAL

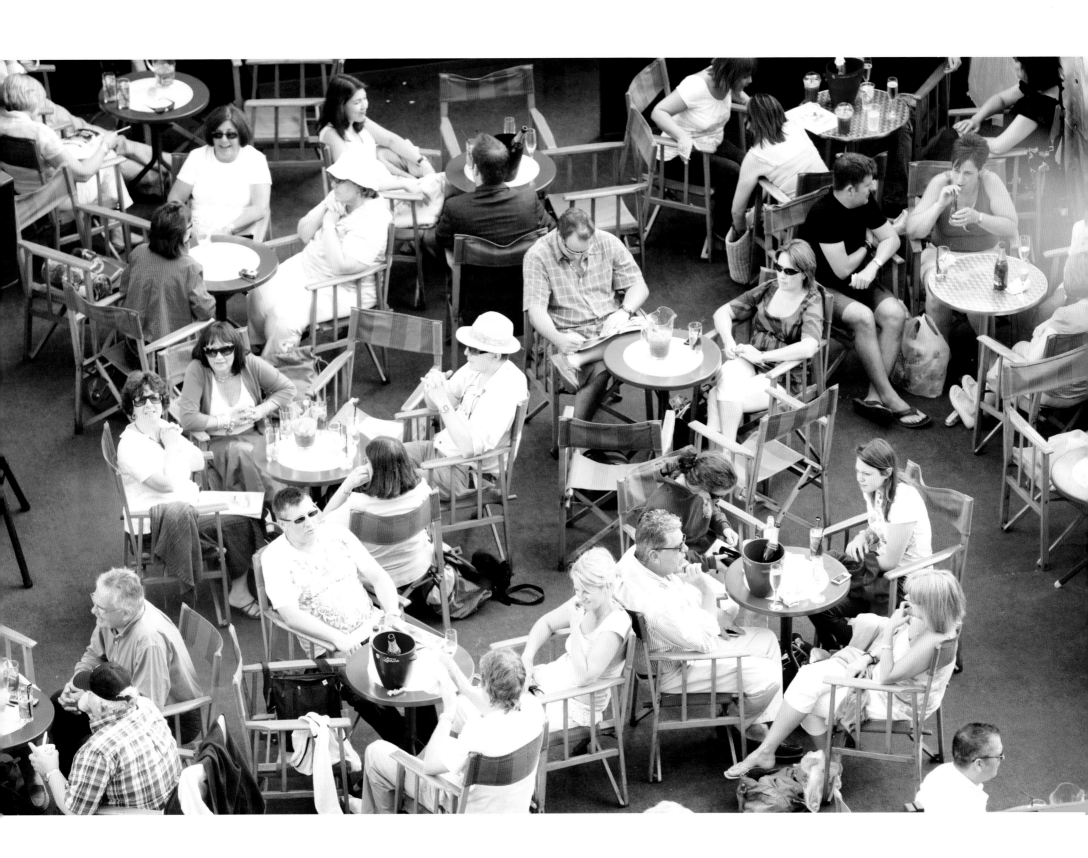

For many, it is time to enjoy a dish synonymous with Wimbledon. Legend has it that the kitchen of Cardinal Wolsey in Tudor times first teamed strawberries and cream together. The dish became popular in the late 19th century, around the time of the start of The Championships – a perfect combination

(above) A jazz band plays for spectators near the popular Pimm's and Champagne Bar, while a number of the public enjoy the surroundings of Café Pergola with its distinctive and cooling fountain.
(right) Centre Court debenture-holders savour a splendid view of the outside courts

Spectators enjoy rest and refreshment under the dappled shade of flower-covered arches in the northern part of the grounds

(above) Andy Murray is
well-supported by family
and friends, including
footballer David Beckham

(right) Rafael Nadal springs
to greet Andy Murray at
the start of their semi-final
in 2010

(above) Enthusiastic
fans show support for
Britain's leading player

(right) Andy Murray
shows determination and
turn of speed

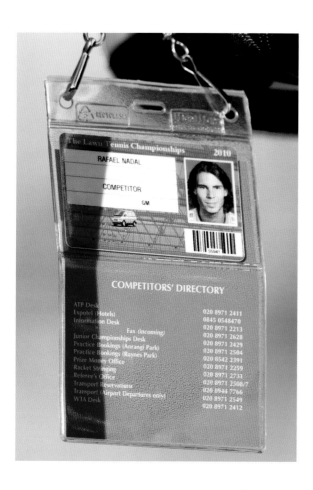

(above) Even the greatest
players need a player's pass...

(above) ...not to mention
their own branded shoes

(right) Rafael Nadal, intent
on victory, is a formidable
competitor

Ball boys are fit,
focused and standing
to attention – but still
with an admiring glance
at a great champion

Late afternoon is, for many, a time to rest and recuperate. **(far left)** Nevertheless, a number of Chelsea Pensioners show typical stamina and fortitude. **(top)** Vera Zvonareva and Elena Vesnina take the opportunity to towel down during a doubles match. **(left)** Other spectators find a good spot for a well-earned rest

RAIN AND THE ROOF

Court coverers are at the ready and then come the gloomy words: "Play is suspended". Unfortunately, this has been a not infrequent announcement over the years – until Wimbledon revealed a new retractable roof over Centre Court in 2009. Scarcely a drop of rain fell during the next two Championships!

A rain delay brings its own Wimbledon activity and atmosphere. Spectators scurry to find cover. Patient fans huddle under colourful umbrellas. The bars begin to fill and the retail shops are busy with trade. The museum, a year-round attraction, is full of visitors absorbed by the treasures of Wimbledon's history.

Since 2009, though, the retractable roof enables play to continue on the grass of Wimbledon's centre stage – and a live tennis experience can be enjoyed by others on screens around the grounds and by millions of television viewers worldwide.

The Centre Court's scheduled programme of play for the day can also be completed if bad light ensues.

The majestic and innovative structure has, for many, added to the grandeur of the world's most famous tennis theatre.

A new experience has been created.

(above) A rainbow brightens the rain-filled sky behind St Mary's Church

(left) Umbrellas are the order of the day during a Wimbledon rain-break

(right) A darkened sky casts its gloom over Wimbledon in 2008

(left) Spectators and staff struggle to seek shelter under any available cover. (above) Fred Perry, still determined, takes the rain in his stride

(far left) Spectators huddle under colourful umbrellas during a rain delay in 2008

*(above) Mopping and sweeping after a
rainstorm. (far left) It is good news for spectators
when the court covers are deflated*

*Spectators, in 2008, watch the desultory scene
from Aorangi Terrace on the large TV screen*

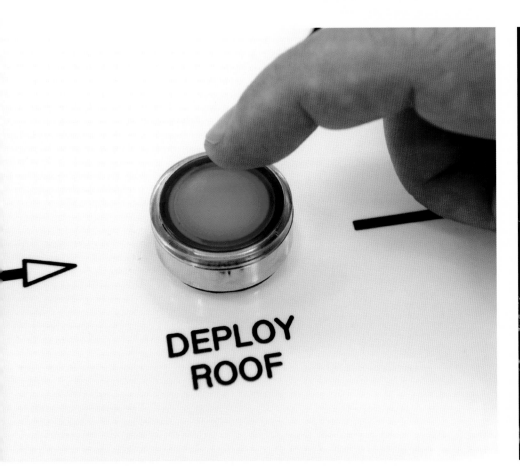

DEPLOY
ROOF

(left and above) Since 2009, the retractable roof on the Centre Court can be used to overcome the rain (or, if necessary, bad light) and so complete the day's scheduled play. The roof closes in less than 10 minutes, the airflow system brings the air circulation and humidity to an appropriate level and play can recommence, on a perfect grass surface, within around 30 or 40 minutes of stoppage. The instruction to close (or open) the roof is given by the Referee

(far left) Play takes place under the Centre Court roof in 2010

(left) Third-seeded Novak Djokovic leaves the Centre Court after completing a five-set victory over Olivier Rochus moments before 11pm – the latest-ever finish at Wimbledon

(overleaf) Outside, the Centre Court roof shines proudly in the night sky while play takes place

EARLY EVENING
TO DUSK

6pm-11pm

As early evening approaches, Wimbledon experiences a fresh surge of interest and activity. When spectators leave, others arrive – some after a long wait, others after a day at work in or around London. Wimbledon's ticket resale operation for the show courts is in full swing. There is still plenty of tennis to see and enjoy. A prime match is often tensely poised on the Centre Court. Shadows slowly fall across the courts. On a warm, sunny evening the light is golden. For many, this is a special time at Wimbledon.

Perhaps it is an opportunity to enjoy a Pimm's or glass of champagne and to listen to the evening band by the Champagne Bar. The Wimbledon shops enjoy bustling trade. In the Media and Broadcast Centres, the press write their reports and television stations around the world prepare their summaries of the day's play. Leading players (and some less well-known enjoying the limelight of victory) give their press conferences. Some of the players are reflective and disappointed; others are positive and hopeful of further progress.

On the outside courts, many matches are still being fiercely fought to a conclusion, the eyes of the players sharp with concentration and spectators unwilling to leave until the battle is won or light finally fades.

Over in Wimbledon Park, the Queue has already started for the following day.

(previous page) Evening casts its lengthening and distinctive shadows. The player is Spain's Pere Riba-Madrid

(right) Low evening sun reaches into the precincts of Court 1 near Aorangi Terrace

(left) As spectators leave, many within the grounds take advantage of buying show court tickets which become available through Wimbledon's unique ticket resale operation. Tickets are resold from a kiosk (situated north of Court 18). All proceeds are donated to charity. HSBC, the banking partner of The Championships, kindly donates a matching amount. In 2010, more than £200,000 was raised

(far left) The early evening sun leaves an oval spotlight on Court 1 as Alejandro Falla battles against Roger Federer in a first-round match

(right) A sign discourages those tempted to bathe in the water garden high on Aorangi Terrace

(far right) A tense evening match can attract huge crowds of viewers in front of the large TV screen on Aorangi Terrace (popularly known as Henman Hill). Approximately 3,000 people are able to watch the action

(overleaf) Rafael Nadal, majestic and focused, is spotlighted on the Centre Court stage by the evening sun

The All England Lawn Tennis Club
Deep Water
No Bathing

(right) British supporters, packed on Aorangi Terrace, watch the large TV screen animatedly as Andy Murray does battle on Centre Court

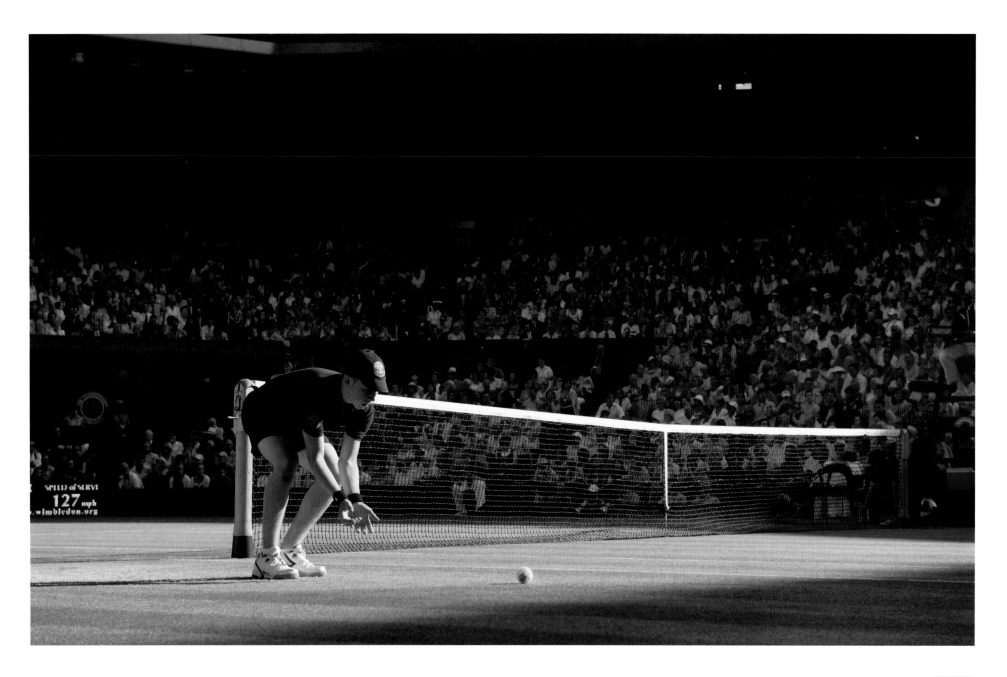

(above) Ball boys and
girls continue to work
with concentration
and skill

(right) Photographers in the
Centre Court 'pits' have Andy
Murray in focus. Around 200
are accredited each year for
approximately 100 international
publications and agencies

(far right) Evening shadows lengthen as the marathon match in 2010 between John Isner and Nicholas Mahut continues on Court 18. (right) The umpire, Mohamed Lahyani, remains in full control

The evening sun falls behind the Millennium Building as a mixed doubles match entertains the crowd in the golden light

Silhouettes and
shade blend in the
evening light

The sun and shade
make a perfect picture
as Vera Zvonareva
shows poise and
concentration during an
evening doubles match

Ball boys and girls remain fit,
ordered and immaculate in
the evening sun

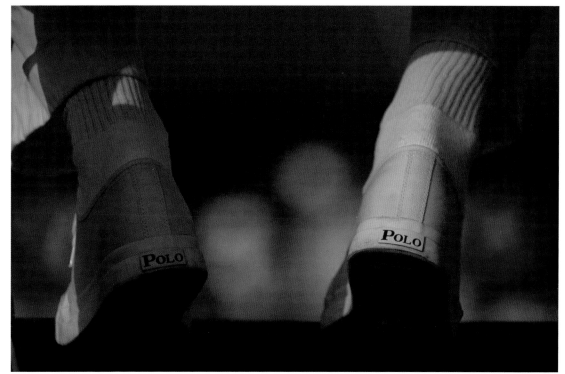

(above and right) Legwear and footwear are spotlighted in the glow of the evening

(far right) Anastasia Pivovarova and Maria Sharapova shake hands. The day's play is over

The match is over and Rafael Nadal **(left)** and
Andy Murray **(above)** face the world's sporting
journalists in the main press conference room
in the Broadcast Centre. Around 725 writers and
radio reporters, from more than 45 countries,
typically attend The Championships

Dusk falls and play
has been completed
for the day. The courts
rest and enjoy watery
refreshment

In Wimbledon Village, the
streets, bars and restaurants
are bustling with evening
activities. The Wombles appear
to have joined the party scene

FINALS DAYS

There is a special atmosphere on the two finals days at Wimbledon. They are the pinnacle of the tournament and, for very many worldwide, the pinnacle of the tennis year.

The Centre Court is the principal theatre. The band plays for early arrivals. The players walk out on to the court at exactly 2pm and the crowd rises in applause and anticipation.

Everyone is in their place. The coin is tossed and the contest begins between two of the world's finest players. They compete in the final challenge for the game's most coveted title until the last point is won. After the last rally is played, quietly and quickly, the carpet is rolled out. The ball boys and girls form two

perfect lines and the Duke of Kent leads the presentation party. The champion is crowned and celebrates with his or her lap of honour to public acclamation.

Titles are decided in the doubles events and, elsewhere, important finals are played in the junior tournament as well as the invitation senior doubles and the wheelchair event. The final of the mixed doubles brings play on the Centre Court to an end. Wimbledon is over for another year.

Ball boys and girls, umpires and line officials all form perfect lines as the presentation takes place

The coveted men's singles trophy (right) gleams in the sunlight

A military band entertains on Centre Court prior to play on both finals days. Playing with gusto here in 2010 is the Central Band of the Royal British Legion

(overleaf) The two finalists are escorted from the changing rooms, walk down the stairs into the entrance hall of the Clubhouse, pass under Rudyard Kipling's famous lines and enter Centre Court for the final contest; Serena Williams and Vera Zvonareva (left), and Rafael Nadal (right). The players arrive at the court at exactly 2pm

The action is fierce and determined as players strive
to gain the sport's ultimate prize. Serena Williams

(left) and Rafael Nadal (right) enjoy a winning
moment and the scent of victory

The moment of victory in 2010 is beautifully captured for Serena Williams (right) and Rafael Nadal (overleaf). Is this moment the pinnacle of the sport?

Roman Zoltowski (above), from Poland, leads a small team of engravers who quickly and skilfully engrave the trophies with the name of the new winner as soon as the final has ended. The winner of the ladies' singles receives (right) a silver gilt salver often known as the Venus Rosewater Dish. The names of the winners from 1884-1957 are engraved on the inside, while those from 1958 onwards go on the outside

(far left) The presentation is a proud and exciting moment – not only for the players but all involved. The custom is for the presenter of the singles trophy (for many years, the Duke of Kent as the Club's President) to be accompanied by the Chairman and Chief Executive of the All England Club and the President of the Lawn Tennis Association

(overleaf) Rafael Nadal, the champion, returns through the Clubhouse under the watchful eye of the Club's Chief Executive, Ian Ritchie, to show the trophy to the waiting crowd at the entrance to the Centre Court building

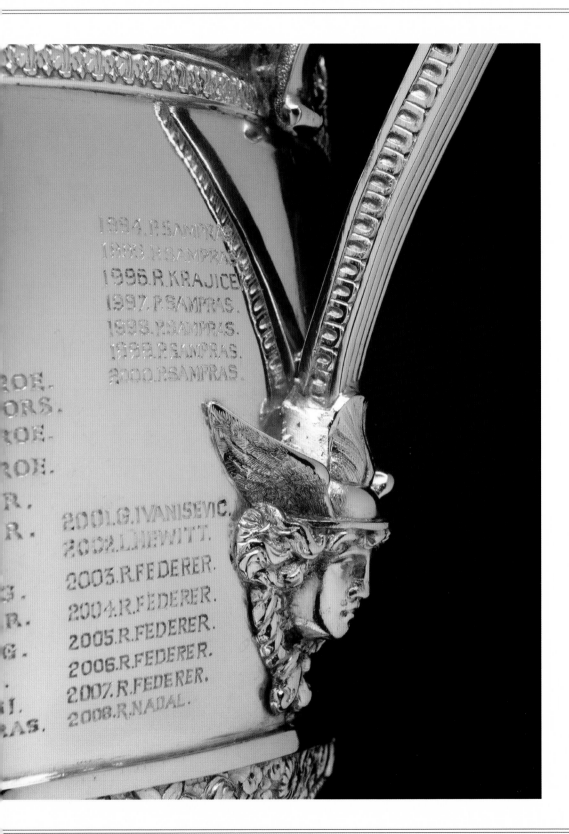

After 2008, there was no room left to engrave any more names on the men's Challenge Cup (left and above), presented to winners of the men's singles final since 1887 after earlier trophies had been retired, so a new plinth was designed to accommodate future champions. The trophies are kept permanently at the Club with each singles winner receiving a fully-engraved, three-quarter size replica

Rafael Nadal (left) and Serena Williams (above)
greet the crowd, each proud to be the 2010
singles champion

The two finals days are occasions for triumph in other important events. Here, in 2010, Sloane Stephens and Timea Babos win the girls' doubles, Philipp Petzschner and Jurgen Melzer are victors in the men's doubles, and Stefan Olsson and Robin Ammerlaan celebrate success in the men's wheelchair doubles event

(far right) Champions Rafael Nadal and Serena Williams, each with their trophy and finely dressed, celebrate at the Champions Dinner, held at a hotel in central London, late on the closing day of The Championships

WIMBLEDON
AT NIGHT

Midnight

The energy-filled action of the day's tennis at The Championships is over. All spectators have left. Behind the closed doors of the All England Club, management and officials have finished a late drink or supper. Thoughts turn to the following day.

Fred Perry's statue is alive with background light as if Britain's great champion of the past is ready to play again. The grass courts enjoy a period of well-deserved rest and revival after the vigorous contests of the day. Buildings glow in the night sky as if on show with festive lights. All, for a few hours, is peaceful and serene. Yet, the grounds of the All England Club still radiate an impressive beauty and grandeur.

Each year Wimbledon crowns its champions and leaves, indelibly and colourfully, its own memories. When night's curtain finally falls at the end of The Championships, the All England Club will revert to being a private members club – proud to have hosted the world's premier tennis event. Planning commences for the following year's Championships.

(previous page) The night sky glows over Wimbledon. A floodlit St Mary's Church is still a distinctive presence. All is set fair for the following day

(right) Fred Perry's statue is backlit amid the glow from the east side of the Centre Court building. His famous forehand is again ready to strike

The Centre Court building is aglow and, with the aid of a long exposure of the camera lens, cars create a blur of light as guests are driven away after an evening party held at the Club during The Championships

(right) Centre Court is empty and still

(far right) The moonlit sky, enhanced by the exposure of the camera lens, casts a dramatic glow on the world's most famous tennis court

(above) Night lights catch the wrought-iron gates of the All England Club, now closed

(right) The lights reflect on the familiar ivy on the outside of Centre Court and the Clubhouse still has a warm and majestic appearance as the clock passes midnight at the All England Club

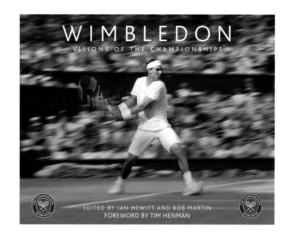

Published by Vision Sports Publishing Limited in 2011

ISBN 13: 978-1907637-12-4

The All England Lawn Tennis & Croquet Club
Church Road, Wimbledon
London, SW19 5AE
www.wimbledon.com

Vision Sports Publishing Ltd
19-23 High Street, Kingston upon Thames
Surrey, KT1 1LL
www.visionsp.co.uk

All pictures: Copyright The All England Lawn Tennis & Croquet Club
Photography by: Bob Martin, Tom Lovelock, Matthias Hangst, Chris Raphael, Neil Tingle,
Tommy Hindley, John Buckle and Steve Wake
Front cover: Chris Raphael
Back cover: Thomas Lovelock

Edited by: Ian Hewitt and Bob Martin
Editorial consultant: Jim Drewett
Design: Neal Cobourne
Sub-editor: John Murray

Printed in China by Toppan Printing Co